TRUST*worthy*

HELEN STEWART

WESTBOW®
PRESS
A DIVISION OF THOMAS NELSON
& ZONDERVAN

Scripture taken from the Holy Bible, NEW INTERNATIONAL VERSION®.
Copyright © 1973, 1978, 1984 by Biblica, Inc. All rights reserved worldwide.
Used by permission. NEW INTERNATIONAL VERSION® and NIV® are
registered trademarks of Biblica, Inc. Use of either trademark for the offering
of goods or services requires the prior written consent of Biblica US, Inc.

WestBow Press books may be ordered through booksellers or by contacting:

WestBow Press
A Division of Thomas Nelson & Zondervan
1663 Liberty Drive
Bloomington, IN 47403
www.westbowpress.com
1 (866) 928-1240

ISBN: 978-1-4908-8036-5 (sc)
ISBN: 978-1-4908-8035-8 (e)

Library of Congress Control Number: 2015907486

Print information available on the last page.

WestBow Press rev. date: 6/11/2015

Contents

Preface

"Helen, you should write a book!" my brother Jim said after I'd shared the latest working of God in my life. I smiled to myself but quickly forgot about it. Then one day my mother said that I should write a book. I forgot about that, too. Then, during a prolonged time of unemployment, I decided to write the times in my life that God met me in my need as a remembrance of God's love and provision for me as His child. I asked Him to bring to mind these various times when He showed Himself to me that I might be encouraged in my faith as I trusted Him to lead me in my job search.

I began to write these stories down and was amazed at how easy it was to write these experiences, feeling the impact as I was, once again, in that very moment. After writing a good number of them, a job possibility opened up that was a perfect next step for me in my career as an interior designer. However, to the amazement of all of us involved, the door suddenly closed. I found out why later on. It is one of my stories. I originally wrote these to encourage my own faith, but when my brother Jim died—leaving three young children behind—I thought these might be an encouragement to them as they learned to trust in the Lord regarding their own lives. Perhaps they will be an encouragement to you as well.

Trust in the LORD your God with all your heart and lean not unto your own understanding, in all your ways acknowledge Him and He shall make your paths straight.

Proverbs 3:5-6

Come, my children, listen to me; I will teach you the fear of the LORD.

Psalm 34:11

The LORD My God

Jehovah *Eli*

The LORD is my rock, my fortress and my deliverer; my God is my rock, in whom I take refuge.

He is my shield and the horn of my salvation, my stronghold.

Psalm 18:2

I am the LORD your God, who brought you out of Egypt, out of the land of slavery.

Exodus 20:2

"Do you have faith?" my dancing partner asked me.

Surprised, I asked, "Faith in what?" Then I said, "Faith in God, yes," and smiled.

We talked a bit more. I was at my square-dancing class. I love to dance, and square dancing was fitting the bill for me. I'd been at it since September, and we only had three more months to go. The calls were getting more complicated and faster. It was so much fun! I smiled and laughed, and laughed some more when mistakes were made.

As one fellow dancer said, "It is a two-hour period of time you can think of nothing else because you have to concentrate so on the calls."

He was right. What a fun time.

The world was getting crazier. Earthquakes and other natural disasters were becoming more frequent and occurring on larger scales. Political tension in the Middle East was increasing daily. Terrorism was worldwide with anti-Semitism growing more rampant. Christians were being martyred in the greatest numbers ever. The economy was not really improving. People in this country were discouraged and afraid. There were wars and growing rumors of more war. Young people with college degrees were unable to find work in their fields of choice or even decent-paying jobs. And the list went on.

As I was moving around my square, following the weaving of the calls, I thought how relaxed and at peace I was in all the movement of the dance. Smiling, I thought that this was just how our God, the God of Abraham, Isaac, and Jacob, wanted His children to be: trusting. Trusting in the love and wonderful grace He showers upon those that believe in Him. Only when we rest in shalom, His peace, amid all the chaos, dissension, trouble, and uncertainty of this world moment by moment, day by day, can we see the beauty of His plan for His followers.

"Yes," I said as I smiled. "I have faith. I have faith in a most loving, great God." I was surprised he asked but thankful he noticed the touch of God on my life.

"Put your yellow boots on today," the still, small voice said as I was getting dressed to go to work. I went into the kitchen to make my breakfast and then finished getting ready for work.

As I was brushing my teeth, I heard once again, "Wear your yellow boots."

As I walked to my front door, I passed my living room and looked out the sliding-glass door. It looked overcast and gloomy. I put on my coat and totally forgot my yellow boots. Opening the door, I threw my bag over my shoulder and ran down the steps.

"Your yellow boots," I heard again.

Oh, I'm running late. I'll be okay, I thought.

As I reached the bottom stair, I stepped onto the sidewalk, and my feet flew out from under me. Ouch! I had tried to brace myself with my left hand as I fell. Sigh. I hadn't listened! I'd forgotten to wear my yellow boots! Here I had been asking the Lord to be sure of His still, small voice. I wanted to know it. I really wanted to do what He said. And here I'd heard it all morning as I was getting ready for work. But I hadn't obeyed. I hadn't really paid attention. He'd been telling me to wear my yellow boots, and I'd just ignored His voice— His warning. He'd known how icy it was and wanted to protect me. My yellow boots were great. They gave me real surefootedness. They were safe to wear on ice and fun in snow. I just didn't slide or fall with them at all.

What a lesson for me. I'd broken my wrist when I could have been safe. I hadn't listened to the Holy Spirit prompting me.

The LORD My Strength

Jehovah 'Ez-Lami

The LORD is my strength and my shield; my heart trusts in him, and I am helped.

My heart leaps for joy and I will give thanks to him song.

Psalm 28:7

Be strong in the Lord and in his mighty power.

Ephesians 6:10

Tears streamed down my face. I didn't know what to think. I could tell it was difficult for my boss to tell me; we were friends. I went to my desk and cleaned out all my things. He left the building. I could have just left, but I wanted to leave everything in good order for the next person. I said good-bye to my coworkers and went home. This job was my first as an interior designer. I was in a daze and needed to think things out.

I had recently found a pretty lake that had a path around it, so I decided to go take a walk and try to think things through. I found the path and started walking, concentrating on putting one foot in front of the other. Tears streamed down my face again. He'd said it just wasn't working; I wasn't fast enough. I'd had a strong desire to be in the field, but maybe I didn't have what it took. Was my dream supposed to stay in dreamland and never become reality? I didn't know where I was going, as I didn't see anything around me, but somehow my feet stayed walking on the path.

Oh, God, help me. I just don't know what to think about all this or what to do.

For days and weeks, I would retreat to the path by the lake and walk out my frustration. I would cry out to the Lord, seeking direction. My confidence in myself had been crushed. I doubted my abilities and questioned my desires. I chose to go in a new direction, to learn some new skill. My heart was not in it, but it was good to learn something new. That in itself helped my confidence improve. I continued to go on my seven-mile walks. At first, I never noticed the trees along the path. I just knew I walked in kind of a tunnel. But as I would walk out my frustration, talking to the Lord, near the end of the walk I was able to focus on one tree. My walk would start out fast and end fast.

Through the weeks of turning to the Lord in my frustration, good things happened. I became very physically fit! I was also having some fun disciplining myself in learning some new skills. Most importantly, I was finding a new joy in the Lord! I was learning to trust in Him in a new way. I was beginning to focus on who He was and is and not dwell on my distress. I began singing praise songs to Him for His goodness to me. My understanding of His love for me grew deeper. Three months later, I was able to walk along the path and look at the beauty of individual trees and notice little flowers poking their color and fragrance out in unlikely places. I had made good progress.

Can this be happening again? I can't say I've felt fulfilled using these new skills, and I've never lost the feeling that I might not measure up like I'm supposed to and be asked to leave again. But I thought I was doing okay.

Well, Lord, You got me through this awfulness once before, I know You can again.

Little did I know, but the Lord had a most wonderful plan in store for me! He knew I wasn't using my talents and wanted to get me to not run away from them in my fears. So, in the only way He can, He brought together all the resources needed to help me get back on the dream track and to begin to, once again, use my talents and abilities as an interior designer. I began with fear and trembling, but I was singing praises to the Lord along the way. It was a slow process but a steady one. Well, mostly steady. My confidence and belief in myself grew as I was able to use my abilities the way I knew I could. I found that I truly believed God was indeed in control, and was I glad! Praise songs to Him became my daily worship.

It had become my favorite song. Michael Card had a way of making my feelings find words. I never got tired of playing it and singing along, even though I'd often feel tears welling up in my eyes. The phrase "though your life may seem to sound of dark and minor key it will soon shift to major" in the his song, "Hope" resonated with me.

Work certainly had not been fun lately, or for a long time for that matter. I had such hopes in coming to work here. I had moved to be closer to my work and not have a long commute. One by one, the fire of each hope had been extinguished.

I had been looking for another job for over a year now. Yet each time I interviewed, I found myself telling the Lord it was all right if He wanted me to stay where I was, if I would bring Him more glory and honor. I knew now that I was to learn some important lessons.

I'd recently been reading the Book of Job. My thoughts went to what Job was going through and it was clear that my struggle was nothing compared to the situation of Job's. Even so, the words of this song held such meaning and gave me strength to continue to trust in the Lord even in this unhappy time. Michael's song continued to speak to me in his words "the lyric of your life will rhyme with nothing less than joy when you find that hope is from the one that you believe." Even though I did not understand just what I was to learn, I was reminded of the Bible verse in Isaiah 40:31 once again. It said, "those who hope in the Lord will renew their strength." I had come to know without any question years ago that God was definitely trustworthy. He alone was my joy, my strength and the only one in which to place my hope.

The LORD Is with You

Jehovah 'Immeku

When the angel of the LORD appeared to Gideon, he said, "The LORD is with you, mighty warrior."

Judges 6:12

"The virgin will be with child and will give birth to a son, and they will call him Emmanuel"—which means, "God with us."

Matthew 1:23

I tossed and turned. I just couldn't get any sleep.

Why don't they talk to me? I wondered. I'd been there a week, and no one would say hello, much less look at me. I didn't get it. I smiled at them as they passed my area. Breaks were just awful. We had to take two fifteen-minute breaks a day. I didn't mind that, but…guess I'll bake some cookies and take them in and offer one to each of the guys.

Lord, help me. I only want to honor You.

Thanks, Lord, the cookies seemed to help some. I was the only girl working there with about fifteen guys. I thought that they'd like that. I thought it could be fun! As the days passed, a couple of the brave ones stopped by my desk and chatted. Slowly they were warming up to me.

Then it happened. One of the guys looked out the window and whistled. He called a couple of his buddies over. Liking to be part of the action, I got out of my chair and went over to the window, too. I smiled. She was a knockout!

"You've got good taste," I said. I then went back to my chair and started working again. I looked up from my work and found them staring at me so I smiled back at them. Then I found out. They had heard before I started working there that I was a Christian. I sighed.

They must have had bad experiences with Christians, I thought. *Well, I'm certainly not going to preach to them. I'm just going to be nice to them.*

That was easy to say and actually easy to do. I learned as time went on that they were quite loveable. As time passed, they became less timid around me and started talking to me. I was glad.

I've always gotten along with men. I guess it has a lot to do with the fact I had a good relationship with my father and two brothers. Most of these men were married. I was in my late twenties at the time and feeling lonely. I wanted a special friendship with someone of the opposite sex. So when one of them mentioned doing something with him, I knew how very vulnerable I was.

Lord, I need to take a stand here. Help me be gentle and kind in how I do it.

They didn't realize how very vulnerable I was! Five of the men I got to really know best. I liked them. They were nice men. However, I started to see a pattern develop. I'm sure they weren't even aware of what was going on. One would come up to me quietly and ask me to do something with him. I would smile and start to ask about his wife. A day or two would go by and another one would come up to me and mention doing something with him. I would smile and mention something about his kids. This would happen until all five men had approached me. Then a few days would go by and the whole process would start over again. I'm sure no harm was really meant by them, but I wasn't taking any chances. I was just too vulnerable and didn't want to dishonor the Lord in any way, not even the hint of possibility.

One of the men wanted to play tennis with me. I was always looking for a tennis partner. But when I explained that I didn't think his wife would like me to play tennis with him, he didn't give up. Soon, he had organized a team. Yes, we played once a week and had a great time. Then, during break, four of us began to play cribbage. It was an ongoing contest. I loved it! Such fun we had.

One night, I was telling one of my girlfriends from church about the work situation. She was horrified and said it was such a difficult situation to be in. Knowing that she was referring to the somewhat constant testing of whether I would succumb to the various invitations, I began to shake. I could not stop shaking as I thought about how much I needed the Lord's strength to withstand the attention these men were offering me, whether in seriousness or jest. Then, I thought how close the Lord was with me in guiding me in what to say and how to say it. I was then able to regain my composure.

One of my new friends at work that played tennis and cribbage with me was battling a certain type of cancer. I was concerned that he would come to know my friend Jesus personally. When I found out he did, I was thrilled. In time, he and I would talk of heavenly things. The other guys didn't like it. They were uncomfortable. But my friend at work would start up the conversation first, and we'd have a good time discussing angels and other heavenly things. In time, the others would come and listen to our conversation. It was very satisfying. He seemed to need to talk about facing death, dying and the blessed hope he had in his future as a result of his faith in Jesus the Son of God with his friends. I was glad to be a part of his life in that way.

A few months later, I was given an opportunity in the big city of Washington, D.C. So saying goodbye to my friends, I moved on to a new experience. I look upon that time in my life as something very special. The Lord was definitely with me, and I could stand firm in a kind way for the principles my Lord, the Rock, teaches.

"Helen, I can't remember names!" Mother exclaimed. "I don't know what is wrong."

I had noticed that her speech was slurred as if she were drunk. *That would be the day!* I chuckled to myself. *She doesn't even drink coffee!*

I was so glad to see her finally. I hadn't been able to leave work since her terrible bone-shattering fall six months ago. She was out of rehab and back into her cottage after valiantly, steadfastly working to get her strength up once again. She now had a walker—actually called a Rollator, as it had four wheels.

I remember the call clearly. She was being flown to a brain trauma unit as she had blacked out, fallen, hit her head, and broken her femur. I called her immediately, and we talked, although she doesn't remember the call. She was so funny. We laughed and laughed on the phone. She now says she thought everyone was talking in Spanish. But now, seeing her, I was troubled.

What was going on? I wondered. I made a call for a doctor's visit. Thankfully, she could see him within the two weeks I was visiting. Her doctor only took her vitals and said good-bye. I was aghast! He didn't even talk or listen to her many questions, and I had promised I wouldn't say anything.

Two days before I left, she had two ministrokes. I was clearly concerned. My vital, quick, and clear-thinking mother was a different woman from only six months ago.

While back at work, I looked something up and ordered a book to be sent to Mother's address. I hoped it would get there in a week.

I arranged to take a month off work so I could observe Mother. As soon as I arrived back at her cottage, the book was waiting. Gathering all her medications, I read about each one in the book and how they interacted with one another.

"Thank you, Lord. I found it." Two pills she was taking were never to be taken together. I'd have bet that's what was causing the problem—and sure enough, it had been.

The LORD Will Provide

Jehovah *Jireh*

So Abraham called that place The LORD Will Provide. And to this day it is said, "On the mountain of the LORD it will be provided."

Genesis 22:14

"I am the good shepherd. The good shepherd lays down his life for the sheep."

John 10:11

"Hello. I was wondering if you still had the kindergarten teaching vacancy. I would like to have an interview," I said.

"Well, it still is open, although we have an interview in a couple of days," mentioned the administrator of the school.

"When could I talk with you about the position? I could come tomorrow."

"Well, I suppose you could interview. We're pretty well decided on this person who's coming. If you really want to come, come the same day, and you can interview then."

"Thank you. I'll be there."

I didn't really think much more about the coming interview as my mother and I planned to make the drive together. It was only about an hour from my ancestral home, so she knew the way.

I was nervous. I didn't really know what to expect, as this was my first interview to be a teacher. I wanted to be a kindergarten teacher, nothing else. I had loved kindergarten. I had loved my kindergarten teacher. My teacher had been my mother. Through that experience as a young child, learning has continued to be an exciting adventure for me. So I wanted to get kids off to a good start by showing them that learning can be fun, just as my mother had for me. Finding a teaching job was not easy that year. I guess there just weren't that many openings, especially for me, since I only wanted the kindergarten grade. I'd been advised by a few friends and teachers to take anything I could get and not to worry about a particular grade. But I was not to change my course. This was the grade for me.

We arrived after the three-and-a-half hour drive. Mother was good company, but I was a bit tired from the drive. I said a prayer and went in for the interview. Was I ever blindsided! They had both of us together for the interview! They only asked questions of her! My back was up. This wasn't fair. I had come a long way! Then we went on a tour of the school. That was it. As they said good-bye, I turned to the interviewer and said I felt cheated. They had not interviewed me as they said they would. I had driven over three hours for an interview. Finally, a few questions were asked of me. Mother and I drove home. After a couple of days, I called to see if they had made a choice. I was told they had offered the position to the other girl and was waiting on her decision. I then said that I was very interested, and if she didn't take the job, I would.

What craziness, I thought as I hung up the phone.

Then I talked with God. "Lord, You know I'd like to teach kindergarten, You know few jobs are out there, but You also know who the best person is for this job, so I leave it in your hands. May the right person become the kindergarten teacher, and, Lord, as

You know, I don't have time to continue looking for work as I've an obligation this summer that prevents me from doing so, and I have to leave within a week. Thank You. In Jesus' name, I pray."

I'd only been home a couple of weeks and had been hard at work looking for a kindergarten-teaching position. Well, it was in the Lord's hands. I needed to get packing.

Three days later, I got a phone call.

"Are you still interested in the kindergarten position?" I was asked.

"Yes, but you offered it to the other girl."

"She decided not to come here. She wants to look over in the Washington, D.C., area some more."

Oh, I thought. "Yes, yes, I'll take the position and thank you!" *Oh, Lord! Thank You for answering my prayer.*

I guess I was the right person.

T here I was, on all fours, playing with my cat, Tiffany. She was my only cat and the first animal I'd had since a child when our family had a dog. She thinks I am a big cat. I was chasing her, just having a good time, when I heard a knock on the door.

"Oh, Tiffany, someone is at the door." She ran down the hall, and I jumped up to answer the door.

My neighbor stood at the door. She quickly said, "Do you want to go out for a pizza?"

I laughed aloud. "Yes, but are you paying? I don't have any money right now."

She said, "Sure! I just don't want to eat at home and stare at the walls tonight. I need to get out."

"Great, let's go."

That happened on Monday. Little did I know what a wonder that week was going to become. We shared some funny stories, laughed, and thoroughly enjoyed the pizza. We had both been hungry for it.

The next day was my usual swimming night, and it was time to go, so I quickly put on my bathing suit. My swimming partner was soon knocking on my door. It was time to go swim our laps.

"Come on in," I said. When she came in, I looked up from the dining room table and smiled. I felt caught. "I'm just counting my pennies. This is it for two more weeks. It's going to be interesting."

I had just a few dollars to my name.

As we were walking to our respective condos after the swim, my friend kindly said, "Come on over if you need some food or anything. I know what it's like."

"Thanks, that is really sweet," I said. I then found myself remembering a time when I had asked to go to my cousins' house for a meal, as I just needed to be with some family, and how uncomfortable I felt.

No, I thought, *I just won't do that again.*

Wednesday night I received a telephone call from the leader of my church's singles group. I was helping on the committee just then, and we were planning a progressive dinner and deciding who would serve the appetizer, salad, main meal and dessert at each persons' home that was hosting the dinner for Saturday night. As we talked on the phone, I explained my situation and mentioned how I was sorry not to be able to join in on the event. I said that I knew they would all have a great time, and I'd be happy to still help with the planning but just couldn't go to the dinner. She finally persuaded me to come as planned and not worry about the cost. The group would cover me.

How nice of them, I thought. It was so good to know that the singles group was looking forward to my joining in the activity as much as I was anticipating the evening.

Thursday night, as I was waiting to go swimming again, the telephone rang and as I was talking on the phone, a knock was heard on my door. Ending the phone conversation, I opened the door. A man handed me an envelope explaining that he was the husband of my swimming partner. He said his wife wouldn't be going swimming the next week as she wasn't feeling well. I was disappointed. His wife and I always felt so good after the exercise. I said I hoped she would be feeling better soon.

Closing the door, I opened the envelope. Such a beautiful picture of two cats! Underneath, it said, "A friend loves at all times."

How sweet, I thought. Then I opened it up and read: "Hope this helps." There was a twenty-dollar bill. Wow! What a humbling experience!

Saturday, I stood with my jaw down to the floor. I watched as a friend carried in several bags of groceries and put them on my counter. It was enough food for about a month! I was so very humbled and thankful. She didn't say a word. She just fulfilled a need. She understood what it was like. She'd had her own business once, too. Even though my experience qualified for a large hourly rate, I didn't always get the work I needed to make ends meet. I had normal, everyday expenses. She remembered what it was like and had heard me say on the phone the other day that I didn't have any food. I wasn't trying to manipulate her response to my situation. I was just stating a fact as we talked on the phone. Her spiritual ears had heard and she'd responded. She hadn't asked if she could do anything. She had heard and had acted. She'd taken her relationship with Jesus seriously. She'd been the arms of Jesus, showing his love to me by responding to my need. Jesus promises to meet our needs. He did through her. What a blessing to me. What a friend.

Sunday after church, someone I had recently met came up to me and asked if I'd be interested in helping her out with some of her work. Interested, I responded by saying I would love the experience. In fact, it was perfect for the new direction I was going in with my interior design skills.

Later that day I was reflecting on all these happenings. I found my thoughts taking me back to the Sunday before, when I had been meditating on Jehovah *Jireh,* God my provider. He sure had been providing for me in so many beautiful ways this past week. Funny, I hadn't asked Him to provide for me in these ways last Sunday. I had just been meditating on how wonderfully He had provided for me when I was in a similar situation twelve years ago. What a loving way to encourage me at this time, not only financially, but also emotionally and in my new career direction.

I was changing career directions at a time when the economy was in some trouble. In fact, jobs were said to be harder to get now than in the 1990s. I remembered again how He had opened up various doors of opportunity back then as well. What a wonderful caring God my Jehovah is.

"Cow! Moo!," Smiling, I called out to the adorable little puppy. I couldn't remember her name, but she was long-haired, black and white, and made me think of a Holstein cow. Her owner laughed and said my calling her little puppy "cow" was cute. The name stuck.

Loving longhaired animals as I do, I had decided the next animal I'd get would be a dog. I'd need a dog to get me up in the morning and get some exercise as well. My cats were perfect for me now, but as I'd age I figured a dog would be best. Cats didn't need to go outside or take a walk. If I had another cat in my later years, I might stay in bed in the morning and remain lazy all day. Not good. So it was decided. A dog would be next as long as it had long hair. Occasionally, I'd play with what kind it would be but only for an instant. My two adorable Himalayans had years to live, and I loved every minute with Trouble and Mitzie. At least, I thought they had years to live. Trouble died a terrible death at the age of ten. He was my heartthrob! Mitzie finally received the attention she deserved. She was such a perfectly beautiful, sweet cat. But after one-and-a-half years, she died at age thirteen. Having another pet while my mother was aging and needing more attention might be too much for her, so I didn't consider getting one.

Then the Lord gave me inspiration. Cow's owner didn't always feel well. Perhaps she'd let me walk her each day, giving her owner a rest and me some joy. It was all arranged and little Lulu and I happily went on our way. We chased birds, squirrels, saw deer, and rabbits. We ran through the grass. She became my little buddy, giving me some needed exercise and letting my playfulness come alive. This provided a very needed and enjoyable respite of being a caregiver, 24/7. Thanks, Lord!

The LORD Our Guide

Jehovah *Kathegetes*

For this GOD is our God for ever and ever; he will be
our guide even to the end.

Psalm 48:14

"You have one Teacher, the Christ."

Matthew 23:10b

*W**oosh!* I jumped up from my chair on my balcony quickly, walked into my living room, and began to pace.

Lord, what is going on? What do You want me to do? Is there something You want to tell me?

I kept pacing. I kept on praying and listening to hear God's voice.

I had been enjoying the quiet of the morning and thinking about my friend who was giving a flying lesson. He had taken me flying a few times. I loved it. However, I was a bit skeptical to let him show me how the g-force would feel, so we never did anything more than plain, easy flying. He was tons of fun, but when he flew the plane, it was a different story. He was serious about flying, very professional and careful. Then I heard the *woosh* and felt as if I'd been hit by a ball of energy. The air that morning was heavy. I had prayed for my friend while sitting on my chair on my balcony.

Then in the evening, I got the call.

"Hello," I said. "Yes, this is Helen." As I listened to the caller, my heart skipped a beat. He told me that he was calling everybody in the address book, and I was near the last to call. He apologized for calling late into the evening. I then knew what the Lord wanted me to do. Here was my answer to my morning's question. I put the phone back on its cradle and sighed.

Thanks, Lord for telling me what You want me to do.

I prayed. I prayed for my friend's parents and the rest of his family. I knew them. They were friends of mine also. I thanked God that my friend had come back into a relationship with the Lord after wandering far away. I thanked the Lord that I knew he'd found answers to questions that had troubled him for so long. I was thankful that I knew, without a doubt, he was now with Jesus.

So I prayed for the people who would be coming to his funeral. They probably did not know of his new commitment to be in a relationship with the Lord. It all had been so recent, and he'd had so many friends. He had been so full of life. He'd always been clowning around, good at his job while also burning the candle at both ends. I continued to pray that, somehow, at his memorial service, his testimony of trusting in Jesus once again and the peace he'd found would be shared. I prayed that all those remembering him would come away with a fuller understanding of what was most important to him—that life does go on after we die and one's relationship with God's Son continues on in great beauty and joy in God's presence.

The time came for his memorial service. It was a beautiful service and testimony of God's incredible love to us and my friend's response to that love. The Lord not only answered my prayer that day but also showed me how to pray. I was grateful and yet sad to lose my friend for now.

I didn't understand. It didn't make any sense. It was so hurtful. I knew I needed to forgive her. We were commanded to forgive. Tears streamed down my face as I lay on the single bed. Here I was, renting not a room but enough space for a single bed with a curtain from floor to ceiling as my wall. It was a space off the main hall. It was like an alcove that was just big enough for a single bed. It was a lovely old house that had been turned into a boarding house.

Oh, Lord, I know I need to forgive her, but I have no feelings of forgiveness toward her.

My great-aunt lived in the lovely Stewart home with four bedrooms. It had been in our family since 1790, and each generation had added a room to it. I had written her, asking if I could live with her that summer, as I'd gotten a summer job working as a waitress at the historic inn across the street from her house. She'd said yes.

However, when the time came, she'd changed her mind. So I found a bed in the town nearby. I cried myself to sleep that night. I had looked forward to living with her and getting to know her better. She also had been a teacher. I knew I could learn much from her. The expense of boarding took most of my earnings. The lack of real privacy was unnerving. I struggled with being obedient in forgiving her.

A few nights later, with tears again falling down my cheeks, I agreed to forgive her. In my prayer that night, I told my Father God that I forgave her and trusted Him to give me the feeling of forgiveness. And, you know, the feeling came about as I continued to show my great-aunt kindness, and our relationship was restored.

The LORD My Refuge

Jehovah *Machsi*

If you make the Most High your dwelling
Even the LORD, who is my refuge
Then no harm will befall you,
No disaster will come near your tent.

Psalm 91:9,10

You are my hiding place; you will protect me from
trouble and surround me with songs of deliverance.

Psalm 32:7

What's going on? I pressed the accelerator down harder. Still,
there was no get up and go. In fact, I was slowing down even more.

Oh, no. Was I out of gas? I thought for sure I would make it
back to Virginia from the meeting in Maryland fine. It looked like
that was the problem—the gas. I pulled over onto the shoulder of
the road. It wasn't a very good place to stop. There was an overpass
just ahead and an exit just behind me.

*This is just great. Here it is eleven thirty at night, and I'm out of
gas.* I thought I had checked my figures and would be fine. I figured

wrong. My gas gauge had been broken for six months now, and someone had shown me how to keep track of how much gas I was using. It had worked fine until tonight. *Boy, what a time for me to run out of gas!* I took a deep breath and began figuring out all my possibilities. I didn't have any flares. Not smart. I could lock the car up and walk to the nearest house or whatever. I had on a dark coat, and I sure didn't know the area very well at all. I could just curl up and go to sleep. *Ha.* Doubt I'd get much sleep. *Wish I had some flares.* But then you never know who might come up to help some woman in the late hours of the night. What a scary thought.

I stopped thinking and just looked out at the night.

"What am I going to do? Lord, I'm scared. I have on a dark coat, no flares, and I'm stopped in a bend in the road. Not much time for someone to see me and if they did, would I want to see them? Please help me."

I didn't know what to do except to stay with my car and take the risk of flagging someone down.

"Lord, You know who is driving on the road tonight, so will You guide someone to me who will not harm me but help me out?"

All right, I'm getting out of the car. Here I go.

I didn't seem to stand there very long at all when a car pulled over. I got in my car to wait for him to walk up to the car.

"Hi," I said. "Thanks for stopping."

He said he barely saw me until he was right on me. He also said he had promised himself he would never again stop to help someone because the last time he did someone robbed him. I relaxed.

I told him my gas gauge was broken and hadn't fixed it, because there always seemed to be other, more urgent, expenses. Somehow, I had calculated the mileage wrong. He said there was a gas station close to the next exit and he'd go get a gallon to put in my car.

I said, "Fine. And thanks!"

I never thought he wouldn't come back, because I knew the Lord brought him to help me. So I quietly waited as I thanked the Lord for providing the needed help at such a terrible hour.

Before long, he was back. He put the gas into the tank, and then suggested I follow him to the gas station. I did. What a good man. He really went the extra mile for me.

I suddenly woke up. *What was that noise? Where was it coming from?* I sat up and listened some more. I got up and quickly walked to the other side of my little cottage, where the screened-in porch was, and listened again. There was that sound again.

Oh! I rushed to my mother's bedroom and found her holding her head and moaning.

"Mother? What is wrong?" All she could do was moan. I looked around and pieced together her story. It wasn't a pleasant one.

"Lord, what do I do? How can I help her? Please guide me—I need some wisdom."

I put a cold, wet cloth on her head and sat down beside her. She kept on rocking, holding her stomach and her head and moaning. Then the Lord brought to mind a book I'd read some fifty years ago on what drug addicts go through when going through detox.

"Oh, Lord!" I begged. "Please be with her and keep her alive!" *How did this happen?*

We discussed going to emergency, but she was adamant about *not* going. So I did all I knew to do. I sat beside her and prayed for her.

Being a caregiver was a new thing for me. Being rarely sick myself, I didn't know what foods to fix for someone in various illnesses. Cooking three meals a day for a day, week, even a month was overwhelming to me. I'd rather be outside or reading a good book any day before cooking. How I'd managed to eat, being single all these years, was amazing to me, for I was healthy. Yet, with all these new uncertainties, I was so thankful my mother had moved in with me and I could have the special opportunity, and, yes, responsibility of being her caregiver these last years of her life. It was certainly different from calling or visiting in a care facility. Close friends were concerned I would take good care of myself so I could continue to give good care.

"A matter of balance, as always," I'd say.

I felt my life enriched by my mother's presence. We looked at photo albums, she heard me play the piano and my fiddle. It gave her pleasure. We discussed world events. We watched family TV shows neither had ever seen and listened to Christian news reports. I read books on prophecy and shared my learning. I read biographies of her choice to her and so learned things I would never have sought out. We went for walks and drives together. She laughed with me at my cat's antics. She pushed Trouble and Mitzie around on her Rollator. She enjoyed my winter fires, soups, and homemade breads. She endured my cutting her hair. I learned how great she was at detail when I began doing her taxes. My admiration for her doubled in numerous ways when I compiled her stories for her book. But what we enjoyed most was listening to a few excellent preachers on TV and me reading the Bible out loud just before she went to sleep.

All of this I would have missed out on had she not moved in with me. It is so very true that in giving we receive. I'm so humbled and thankful I'd been given this wonderful responsibility to enjoy and care for my mother. Having been such a daddy's girl, it was nice to be given this time to get to know my mother in a different way. It was a wonderful new opportunity to gain a deeper understanding and appreciation of her. It wasn't always easy. We have differences in our humor, different understanding, and different ways of expression and thinking, but we have always had great respect, admiration, and love for each other that undergirds everything.

What a gift not only to have such a sweet, giving, thoughtful, kind and loving mother, but also now the privilege to mirror back to her even a little of what she has given me all my life.

Thank You, Lord! Thank you, Mother!

"Oh, what a beautiful morning; oh, what a beautiful day." The tune of a favorite childhood song went through my mind. It was a beautiful spring day! I opened the closest door and took out my pink knit suit to put on. Pink was my favorite color, and this suit was special. I slipped on the straight skirt and was ready to go. Took a last look in the mirror to make sure all was in order.

Running a bit late, I'd better get going.

Outside I drank in the spring air. As I walked, I couldn't help but hear the birds all singing and see the sun dancing on the leaves. Oh, I felt so alive and to be sixteen as well!

At the corner of the next block, I noticed a man painting outside someone's house. He noticed me as well and called out to me.

"Hi," I replied.

"You sure are pretty," he said.

"Thanks." I blushed. I felt pretty today. My suit seemed to show off my little curves nicely, and, well, it was a beautiful spring day.

"Why don't you come over here and talk to me," he said.

"Sorry, I'm on my way to church." I replied.

"Come talk later, then, after church lets out."

"Well, okay."

He was still there. So I went across the street. We talked for a few minutes, and then I started home.

"Wait, what's your phone number?"

I gave it to him. I don't know why. Maybe because it was a spring day and I was sixteen. I forgot all about it. A few days later, I got a phone call.

Then he said, "Helen, how about meeting me at such-and-such place?"

"No. I'm not allowed to date so why don't you come here?"
Click.

A few more days passed, and I heard from him again. He wanted me to meet him someplace, but I told him he should meet my parents and pick me up at my house. Somehow, I didn't like the sound of this.

Click. He hung up again. Good. That's fine with me. I didn't care.

A couple of weeks later, I was glancing at the newspaper when an article caught my eye. Some guy in a nearby town had raped and killed a local girl.

How awful, I thought. I read on. He was young, married, and sounded just like that painter that had wanted to meet me somewhere! I was dumbfounded. I just sat there looking at the article. I could be mistaken.

No. They had caught him, and the description was just the way I remembered him. That could have been me! My mind went back to that beautiful spring day when I was feeling so flirtatious and we had chatted. I hadn't told anyone about him, and it could have been me! I'm sure glad I obeyed my parents. It did seem strange he wouldn't come to the house.

Lord, thank You for protecting me and guiding my thoughts to obey my parents' rules.

There it was again. It was the same dream. Why was I dreaming the same dream? It was unsettling. I decided to ask the Lord what this dream meant. And so I prayed. As I talked to the Lord, I recalled the dream.

I was driving somewhere, and there was a smell coming from around me. Then I noticed smoke. It started off just a little bit of smoke and then grew in size. I continued to drive, and then there I was, engulfed in a fire!

The dream varied only in the location each time I dreamed. Always, however, there was a fire. I had been having this same dream, night after night, for about three weeks. It was disturbing. Yet I was always driving.

Perhaps something is wrong with my car? I wondered.

I decided to take my car in for a check. But before I got to the appointment with the mechanic, the car slowed down. I pushed the accelerator down, but the car barely moved. It then hit me that perhaps it was the alternator! For some reason I remembered an incident with an alternator years earlier in another car.

Is this the answer, Lord? Is this what You were warning me about in my dream?

I felt a real sense of peace as I finally arrived at the gas station. The mechanic confirmed what the Lord had revealed to me. Such relief! My heart overflowed with thanksgiving as I waited for a new alternator to be put into my car. The Lord had been warning me about my car! My car was not safe. I had finally gotten the message. Oh, His love, mercy, and patience toward His children!

The LORD My Deliverer

Jehovah *Mephalti*

I call to the LORD,
Who is worthy of praise,
And I am saved from my enemies.

Psalm 18:3

Christ has indeed been raised from the dead, the
firstfruits of those who have fallen asleep.

1 Corinthians 15:20

I can't believe it! I'm really here! I was enjoying my lunch of cheese, bread, and an orange with my new friend at the Colosseum. Yes, Rome, Italy. Today was our free day to explore on our own, and we'd decided to come back to the Colosseum. The tour of it had been just too fast. We wanted more time to remember the events of history in this ancient place.

It had already been an adventure getting there with our trusty little Italian dictionary and map. But there we were. I looked around as we ate and noticed a man standing at the entrance of our little alcove, wearing a typical gray suit. What I found interesting was his very colorful tie. We weren't talking, just eating.

Not too long into our respite, I noticed six Italian men walking toward us. Instead of walking past, they surrounded us. Neither one of us spoke. Perhaps we both quietly decided not to give ourselves away by speaking. They didn't need to know we were Americans who couldn't speak Italian. What did they want with us? Why were they surrounding us? Where was that man with the gray suit and colorful tie? He'd been standing still for at least fifteen minutes watching us, but now he was gone as we were encircled.

Suddenly, one man sat down on my friend. I quickly responded by pushing him off. He was way too heavy for her, as she was quite petite, but then, why would he do such a thing?

Still neither of us spoke. All six men started speaking at once. Were they apologizing? Did they think we were homosexuals? Finally, they left.

When we'd finished our lunch and looked around to find no one in earshot, we spoke. We were unnerved. We decided we would take another quick look at the Roman Colosseum and then get a bus. Upon getting on the bus, we heard English. We looked at each other and smiled as we sighed in relief, but then I noticed the man with the gray suit and colorful tie.

Oh no, he's staring at me! I looked away. Whispering to my friend, we jumped off the bus and tried to find a cab. Unable to do that, we began walking. Then I saw him. It was that man again! *Why is he following us?* We had jumped off the bus, but we had been standing right next to the door. He had been three or four people beyond us. She looked on the map to find a police station. We began heading in that direction.

We tried to walk at a normal pace, but I was constantly aware of that man. He stayed at a good pace behind us. Was it only about twenty feet? At last, we saw what we were heading for. Finally, we arrived at the police station. We opened the door and, to our surprise, faced only stairs. We ran up the stairs and then, to our dismay, noticed six doors off the stairwell.

Which door? I started at one end and she the other. Wouldn't you know it—the last door we tried finally did open. We rushed in. Then, with book in hand, she looked up words and tried to speak Italian. One police officer understood and ushered me out onto a small balcony.

"Yes, there he is!" I exclaimed as I pointed to a man walking away from the building. They understood.

Relieved as we felt, we were thankful to be escorted to where the cabs were waiting. The police, having talked with the nuns at the convent where we were staying, clarified for us any questions that were raised.

Just as we were getting into the cab, I noticed him again! *Who was he? Did the police go after him when I pointed him out?* As he'd rubbed shoulders with me, he had been so close. Thanking the police, we were on our way. Our free day had certainly been filled with adventure. I was shaking and so thankful I could talk with my Father without anyone hearing me at any time.

When I got back home in the United States, I told my brother Jim about my scare. He confirmed my fear as he said the Colosseum was a place single women were taken for sex trafficking.

"Thank You Lord, thank You for Your guidance and protection during that escapade."

W*as I dreaming?*

"Helen."

I felt I was in a deep fog.

"Helen, wake up."

I struggled. I pulled the covers over my head. I couldn't get through the fog!

"Helen."

This time I woke up and nearly choked. I was in a fog.

"Oh, Lord," I cried out. "What is going on? What do I do?"

I was looking after my younger cousins in Arizona. We were living in a trailer house, and I was in charge of cooking, cleaning, and being a watchful companion to my uncle's two children. They were with him for the summer. He had taken a night shift at the nuclear power plant as an engineer. I didn't know how he did it. He'd come home when we were up in the morning after breakfast. Then he would take us out on his boat to water ski and swim for the day—not every day, but most of the days. It was a wonderful summer. I even saw a real live roadrunner.

The desert of Mojave had its own beauty. I remember one time we were swimming when the wind came up real strong. Dust was beating down on us and the sand hurt. We took deep breaths and went underwater.

Another time, we stayed out on a little sand island and slept in our bathing suits on the sand. Before finally falling to sleep, we enjoyed the light of the incredible number of stars in the dark night. How many shooting stars there were! It was hard to imagine as so many shot through the sky. We tried to count them, but it was impossible. It was an unforgettable night.

I struggled to my feet.

I've got to get my cousins outside, I told myself. I could barely breathe. I finally got the youngest one up, and with his help, we finally woke his sister up. We then dragged ourselves outside to wait. Was the trailer going to blow up? The smell was awful. The whole trailer was full of smoke. As the saying goes, "You could cut it with a knife."

The Holy Spirit rescued us. He finally got through my thick, foggy head and saved us. The window air conditioner had gone bust and put out the awful smoke. It could have killed us. We waited outside for several hours until my uncle drove up. It was a happy reunion, to say the least.

The LORD That Healeth

Jehovah *Rapha*

He said, "If you listen carefully to the voice of the LORD your God and do what is right in his eyes, if you pay attention to his commands and keep all his decrees, I will not bring on you any of the diseases I brought on the Egyptians, for I am the LORD, who heals you."

Exodus 15:26

The people brought to Jesus all who had various kinds of sickness, and laying his hands on each one, he healed them.

Luke 4:40

How long? How long?
　　How long, O LORD?
Will you forget me?
　　How long, O LORD, will you forget me?
　　Will You forget me forever?
How long will you hide?
　　Will you hide your face?
How long will you hide your face from me?
　　From me?

How long, how long
    How long must I wrestle
    How long must I wrestle with my thoughts
        And every day, every day have sorrow
    How long must I wrestle with my thoughts and every day have
sorrow in my heart?
    Sorrow. Sorrow in my heart?
How long will my enemy
    My enemy triumph
    How long will my enemy triumph over me?
    How long will my enemy triumph over me?
Over me?
Look on me and answer
    Answer O LORD my God. Look on me and answer O LORD
Give light
    Give light to my eyes, or I will sleep
    I will sleep in death.
My, enemy will say,
    I have overcome 'I have overcome him'
My enemy will say, 'I have overcome him,' and my foes will rejoice
    My foes will rejoice.
    Will rejoice when I fall.
But I trust in your unfailing love; unfailing love;
    My heart rejoices in your salvation. My heart rejoices.
I will sing
    Will sing to the LORD, for he has been good
    He has been good to me.
I will sing to the LORD, for he has been good to me.
—Psalm 13

P salm 13 was being read aloud. As it was read in such a manner,
with great anguish and feeling, I found from deep within me a rush

of living water springing forth. I could not stop the tears flowing down my face. It was a cleansing force. I had never heard a psalm read in such a manner. It was a psalm of lament. I was attending a seminary class, as I was hungry to grow in the Lord. I had been dreadfully and wrongfully judged by a Christian group, yes, a body of Christ, and so I looked to God for help and healing.

It was career damaging. I knew I needed to heal if I was to ever be an instrument of God's love and grace to others. Would I ever attempt, once again, to follow God's call? A call that was previously so clear three years earlier, now was a question only my Lord could answer.

Forgiveness is a decision but also a process. The deeper the hurt, the longer it seems to take to complete the process of forgiveness. Grace isn't cheap. God sent His only Son to die in my place by taking my sin upon Himself, so that I could take His righteousness upon me. This was a cosmic activity. Only with His grace can I even attempt to forgive a hurt or injustice.

Oh, the release I experienced in hearing the psalm that spoke to me and my hurt! The cleansing that took place! The healing that took place! It was the final healing.

Oh, how I love my Lord, my God! He heard my cry and as I turned to Him in my distress, He answered by renewing His spirit within me. Praise the Lord, for my spirit can sing once again!

The Almighty God

El Shaddai

"Can you fathom the mysteries of God? Can you probe the limits of the Almighty?"

Job 11:7

And I heard the altar respond: "Yes, LORD God Almighty, true and just are your judgments."

Revelation 16:7

et up."
I tossed around on the bed.
"Find him."
"I don't know how to begin."
"Find him."
"You will have to show me what to do, and where to look, as I've no idea."
"Find him."
"Oh, all right."

I threw my covers off and got out of bed. It was early, earlier than I normally got up. It was the crack of dawn.

"Lord, please help me. Bring to my mind what I need to know to begin my search." *All right, I'll look in my files to see if there is any clue.* I rummaged through file after file looking for a name, something to call out to me. I decided to eat some breakfast and then come back to search some more. At last, I found something that rang a distant bell. It was a long shot but worth the try.

My brother and I celebrated our birthdays a week apart. I was older, but his birthday was a week before mine. We always contacted each other in September. At least one of us did. This year, I hadn't heard from him. I tried calling him on his birthday to no avail. When I didn't hear from him, I thought it odd, but he was a hard one with whom to keep in touch. I pushed it aside.

Then, one day, my brother Jim called to ask if I'd heard from him.

"No, but you know we rarely do," I said. "I'm sure he is off on some lark."

When Mother called to ask if I'd heard from him, I took more notice of us not having heard. I figured he would get in touch when he wanted to. However, I prayed about the situation and let it go.

Well, the Lord answered my prayer by telling me to find him! So I followed one rabbit trail after another until something clicked. I was working at a friend's house, and he could easily see I was upset. I told him the story, and he graciously told me to call any long-distance numbers I needed to until my brother could be found. At last, I made a real connection, then another connection, until I was able to learn my brother's situation. He was in trouble. He needed help and wasn't in a position to find the help he needed.

Why was I the one God used? Of course, the answer was clear. I was available. I was free to go and help out. The rest of our family had responsibilities they couldn't free themselves from. God in his greatness chose me because I was available, although reluctant at first. God answered my brother's deep cry for help by using me. I'm thankful I obeyed. I'm glad it had been my desire for the past year to be aware of God's still, small voice so I could obey and obey quickly, as was my prayer.

I sat shaking, trembling in the church pew. The ushers were walking down the aisle. It was a long aisle, and I was grateful. *Well, was I going to do it? Was I going to trust God in this too?*

I had just taken a new job. It was different from all the others, as it was not a salaried job. I was now earning straight commission. Talk about walking on faith. I was scared. I'd just bought my first home and certainly didn't want to lose it. I was so proud to be a homeowner now. I'd never have been able to own it had I not had help from my parents on a down payment. It was a small, one-bedroom condo. The building had been converted from apartments into condos. I was an end unit with three outside walls, which gave me windows on three sides. I had only one neighbor that butted up to my small kitchen, so I was thrilled. My kitchen was so small that you could stand in the middle and touch all four walls. It was so tiny. But I was now a happy homeowner. Yet it was scary, as I was on straight commission. If I didn't sell, I didn't get paid. If I didn't sell enough, I wouldn't have enough to pay my mortgage.

I learned the importance of putting God first regarding my money, as a small child. Each of us kids had our own set of small, cut-up boxes in which we would divide our allowance. Our allowance was a dime a week. The first box was titled GOD. The second box was titled OTHERS. The third box was titled GIFTS, and the fourth box was titled SAVINGS. The final box was titled MYSELF. Not only was it fun, but also by doing this, we were taught what was priority, even in the use of money. We learned well. All four of us children learned well, as none of us lived beyond our means.

I was beginning to really perspire. My hand was shaking. I had prayed about it the night before and written a check for the tithe, 10 percent of what I needed to earn for the month. This was the first

Sunday of the month. I was serious about this. I wanted to obey the spiritual principle set forth in the Bible. The ushers were now only a pew away. I took a deep breath, swallowed, and put the check into the collection plate. I did it.

"Lord, I am trusting in You for my sales. I'm not going to worry now, because You promise to meet my needs. I know You will bring the clients to me so that my sales will at least be enough to meet my needs. So I thank You ahead of time. In Jesus' name, I pray."

And you know what? He did it! I even became a top salesman—oops—I mean sales*person*.

GOD that Forgave

El Nose'

O LORD our God, You answered them; you were to Israel a forgiving God, though you punished their misdeeds.

Psalm 99:8

God exalted Jesus to his own right hand as Prince and Savior that He might give repentance and forgiveness of sins to Israel.

Acts 5:31

The music started to play. Everybody was standing up. I could hardly breathe. It was so hot, and I felt so heavy. What was that comment he'd said about a shield? I was wearing the necklace that my dad had given me. It was my favorite, but it seemed to be pulling me down it was so heavy. I tried to stand up. People were starting to sing.

They will think something is wrong with me. There now, I was standing. But, oh, I was so tired, and it was so difficult to breathe. *Why is my necklace so very heavy?*

I don't know how I got through that day, or the next few days, for that matter. I didn't start feeling any better, and perhaps that was part of the trouble. I didn't feel much of anything, just a weight and darkness that I couldn't shake off. When I talked to someone, it was as if that person was in another room, even though they were standing right next to me. *What an odd thing.*

I did crazy things, as if I weren't in control of myself. I found I just couldn't sleep at night. The darkness in my spirit and the darkness of the night were just too much for me. I remember lying awake waiting for the first signs of daylight. When morning would come, I was somehow able to drift off to sleep for the first couple of hours of dawn.

I thought of a Christian radio station that played all night. I tuned into it one night out of desperation. I didn't like the music, and the stories just didn't relate to me. I was someone who had asked Jesus to come into my life when I was seven years old. I remember it clearly. I was attending a church camp for one week with my older brother, Jim. It was a lot of fun and especially nice to have my brother there with me, as he looked out for me so lovingly. After a full week of activities, we ended up with a special meeting in which we were all collected into one room and some man talked to us. It was as if I was the only one in the room, and the speaker was just talking to me. What he'd said had sent an arrow into my heart, and when he'd offered to guide us into asking Jesus into our hearts and lives, I'd wanted it.

Afterward, I'd waited until I could talk to him privately, as he had requested anyone that had asked Jesus into his or her life to do. I'd listened to what he'd said and then went back to the cabin I was sharing with the other girls. When I'd come in they were already in bed and noticed my coming in late.

"Yes," I'd told them, "I prayed for Jesus to be Lord of my life." It was a very real and private decision on my part, and I felt uncomfortable telling them, yet it was good to hear myself say it aloud, as it became even more real. I didn't feel any differently, to my knowledge, but the Lord was already teaching me, I could quickly tell.

So, what did the program called *Unshackled* have to say to me? I listened to the story that night. It must have been two or three in the morning. At the end of the story, all I could think of was that the utter darkness and heaviness I kept feeling had to do with a particular guilt in my life. And, oh, did I feel guilty! But the question was could Jesus forgive this too? I mean, I know He came to forgive us our sins, so we could have the kind of life He had created us for, but, really, how could He forgive me of *this*? Not only had I hurt my relationship with Him, but also with other people that I really cared about and loved as well. Surely, this had gone too far. We are told to trust that what He says is true, and He says He came to forgive our sins and to cleanse us from all unrighteousness. Unright living. Unright believing. I had trusted in His forgiveness before, but *this*?

Oh. Well, I will in this too. The least He can say to me is, *Sorry, Helen, this time you went too far.*

"Oh, Lord, will You forgive me? I really hurt You. I've hurt You before, when I haven't chosen to obey You but this—well, this put You on the cross more than the other things. I am so sorry, so ashamed. I don't deserve Your love. I never did, but I need You so much and miss You. It's been so terribly dark without You. What's that You say? I can barely hear You. You say You love me and miss me too? Wow!"

The LORD God of my Salvation

Jehovah *Elohe Yeshu'athi*

O LORD, the God who saves me, day and night I cry
out before you.

Psalm 88:1

Jesus asked. "Who do you say I am?" Peter answered,
"The Messiah (Christ) of God."

Luke 9:20

I had no energy. Time was running out. I lay in bed hoping,
praying for a miracle. I'd been praying for him on and off since
hearing the news. Was it really six years ago? I'd asked the Lord
to guide me in my relationship —it was so casual. Was I pursuing
God enough in this to show me the way? Was my spirit in tune with
His direction? Was it just two days ago when the neighborhood was
covered with a most beautiful blanket of snow? Twelve inches!

My thoughts took me back to that night, when the snow had
fallen all day. I'd donned my ski clothes and walked into the light
and beauty of the freshly fallen snow. It was like I was the only one

awake. Most of my neighbors' lights were off, as they apparently had already gone to bed. Everything was so still. It was just me and my God walking through the neighborhood. I just had to do it. Now was the time; tomorrow would be too late.

I quickly sat down, then lay down, and made a snow angel. It was like a prayer for each person as I went up and down the road making snow angels. I felt very much alive and happy as I walked alone in the solitude of such beauty, thinking how God loves each person so. I could have gone on all night but decided to turn in for the night. I wanted to get up early to shovel my friend's driveway, for I had promised to do so if it snowed. I shoveled half the day and slept soundly that night.

I woke with a start! I saw flashing lights. *Oh no! Could it be?* I jumped out of bed and went to the window. *Oh, Lord! Please don't let him die—not yet. He doesn't know his Messiah!*

I watched, hardly breathing. The medics brought him out. I sighed, as the sheet wasn't covering his head. He looked so pale. I whispered another prayer.

Lord, please let his children see him in time!

I went back to bed, but my thoughts and prayers stayed with my friends.

The doorbell rang. The message was quick and to the point. I went back to bed and continued to pray. Each day my burden for him became heavier. Each day I had less strength, less energy. His children came. I felt time was suspended. I stayed in bed. My prayer changed.

Lord, he has a heart for God but doesn't know his Messiah. Please reveal yourself to him in a vision.

I'd given him a book about the Messiah. I'd heard he was reading it—did he? Did he come to believe? I sensed in my spirit he didn't have much more time.

I continued to plead with God. It was in God's hands.

It was over. He died. A daughter wanted to meet me. Was she a believer?

We both met each other with that question, and then comforted each other and left with peace—Shalom, God's peace.

*H*elp! Oh, Lord, help me!

His hands were around my neck, trying to choke me! Just a few minutes ago, we had been laughing and talking after enjoying a nice meal out at a nearby restaurant. I prayed, asking the Lord to keep me calm and relaxed as his hands tightened on my neck. Then I asked the Lord to protect me and work in him to calm down and get control of himself.

We were friends and had met through our parents. He liked to fly and gave lessons, and I liked to sail, so we had enjoyed sharing our passions with each other. He was a lot of fun, and we would laugh and laugh together. I remember one time I took him sailing, and he was clowning around as usual. I couldn't resist when I noticed he was on deck on all fours, so very near the edge of the boat. So, well, I did what anyone would do in such a great opportunity, I stuck out my leg and pushed him over. I laughed with glee as he came up and the boat was sailing on. He quickly swam over to the boat and pulled himself up and on. We laughed the rest of the day. He could be such fun!

Why was he now trying to hurt me by squeezing my neck? It was such an immediate change from our enjoyable dinner. He was getting married and had taken me out to tell me the news. I was happy for him. We hadn't seen each other since he had met her. We'd never been the so-called boyfriend/girlfriend kind of friends. We were just friends. So why was this happening?

My mind flashed back to another time someone had tried to strangle me. I'd had a rental property and had decided it was time to sell. The townhouse was quite new still, but I could see damage was taking place from the renters. I didn't have the money to do the repair work that would be staring me in the face if things went on as they were headed. I had already reduced the rent to help the renters out. That was a mistake, as they took greater advantage of me.

So one day I called and told them I wanted them to move out on a particular day. Thankfully, they agreed, but I wanted to be sure. So, unable to find a male friend that could go with me to make sure they were moving out, I went by myself.

When the renter saw me, she came up to me angrily and started to choke me. I cried out to God then, to save me from this abuse. He heard my cry, and she released her hands from around my neck and walked away.

Why was he trying to hurt me?

Then, as suddenly as he put his hands around my neck, he took them away. I didn't ask him what was going on. I felt it best to let it alone. So I got out of the car and went to his side. He opened the door, and I reached over and hugged him. I again told him I was happy for him and wished him the best.

I was thankful that I could call on the name of Jehovah, my God, to save me in my time of need. What a Savior, what a friend! He is only a prayer away. I'm so glad that I can rest in His presence in my life.

God of My Mercy

Elohe Chaseddity

Remember, O LORD, your great mercy and love, for
they are from of old.

Psalm 25:6

Praise be to the God and Father of our Lord Jesus
Christ! In his great mercy he has given us new birth into
a living hope through the resurrection of Jesus Christ
(Yeshua ha-Moschiach) from the dead.

1 Peter 1:3

I'd always dreamed of getting married.

That's just the way things are supposed to be, I thought. So why
was I giving my dream up when I had met someone I enjoyed being
around and had respect for? Well, it wasn't easy to give up the
dream. Getting married was long overdue as far as I was concerned.
I wasn't a women's lib type. I'd always felt I was equal to man—not
the same, for sure, but equal. I thought it was great for the man to
go to work and the woman to stay home with the kids. Not that I
didn't believe in using my abilities, but if I was going to have kids, I

wanted to raise them. I believed that was the privilege and pleasure. But then, I didn't have to concern myself with that, as I had just given up my dream.

We were both lonely when we met. He was a great listener; I was the talker. We shared common interests. We loved the outdoors, animals, and water sports. He was a family-type man. I loved my family. He knew how to say how he felt about something and when he needed to be tough or tender. He was thoughtful and kind. He was a hard worker. He knew what it was to take responsibility. We even enjoyed the same kind of movies and food. We enjoyed each other. We were comfortable with each other. He wanted to spend the rest of his life with me, and I with him.

I couldn't. I hadn't meant to lead him on. We were friends.

We were lonely. I'd been new to the area when I'd met him. I'd been finding it difficult to make good friends. He was a good friend to me. I was getting older and really didn't want to be single all of my life. I'd had possibilities before, but I didn't feel they loved me or truly understood what was important to me. My relationship to God was of most importance, and marriage just wouldn't work if he didn't have God as the number-one priority also. It was easier to say no then. So, it was different this time and, still, I had to say good-bye to the dream of marriage.

Because of one small verse in the Bible, I couldn't marry him. It said, "Do not be unequally yoked." It was a command, not a suggestion. I thought that if it was such an important command, then why wasn't it mentioned more than once? I had been trying every which way to wiggle out of this one.

A comment came to my mind that was this: "God only needs to say something once. Just because something is stated once doesn't mean that it is less important than something stated more often."

I thought about all that the Lord had done in my life. He had been so patient with me. He had taught me such wonderful things about who He was and is. I knew He loved me and wanted the best for me. That was it, wasn't it? He wanted the best for me. How could a child of the light live intimately with someone who did not personally know the God of light?

It wasn't that he didn't believe in the God of light. He was a Jew, one of God's chosen people—the people that God chose to bring forth His Son, the light for the world. It was that he didn't personally know the God of light. I would never be known by this man in the area of my life that was of the most importance to me. He was someone who still lived in darkness.

I could marry him, and God would still love me. But it wouldn't be God's best for me. Then I sighed. I wouldn't be my best for God either. By marrying him, my life would show that I hadn't trusted in Him completely, and He was completely trustworthy. I wanted my life to be one of honor and glory to the Lord, for, you see, His love was better than all the silver or gold I could ever want. Yes, even a man's love. Yes, Jesus was the Lord of my life.

The Most High God

El Elyon

Then Melchizedek King of Salem brought out bread and wine. He was priest of God Most High.

Genesis 14:18

Therefore, since we have a great high priest who has gone through the heavens, Jesus (Yeshua) the Son of God, let us hold firmly to the faith we profess.

Hebrews 4:14

*L*ord *Jesus, I need something more. Something bigger than myself and the little world I live in, taking care of my mother every day.*

Then it happened. *Oh, Lord, when we trust in You and rest in Your love and timing in our lives things fall together so beautifully.*

I was invited to a dinner event with some friends. It was fun to be going somewhere and spending time with my new friends. Little did I know how the Lord was guiding my words and opening up conversation with these two couples. A comment was made that could be interpreted as a question, but I decided not to answer. A question was asked of me when we left, and I shared why I was still single. It was a lovely evening, and as I prayed that night, I asked the Lord to lead me in answering his question.

Thanksgiving and Hanukkah were the same day, and Mother and I were invited to celebrate Hanukkah with my new friends. I was thrilled. I intended to answer his question, but the conversation didn't go that way. I'd had a heart for Jewish people for many, many years. Was this an answer to my prayer for reaching out to others from my little world at home with my mother? I prayed daily for guidance in my relationship with my Jewish friends. One night, the Lord gave me an idea. Why not invite them Christmas Eve? Mother agreed to the idea.

I thought about how we would celebrate. How do I best express what Christmas means to me? I spent nights in prayer. I spent days in Scripture. How much do I share? Little by little, my thoughts became clearer. Everyone was coming! I was thrilled as even my Jewish neighbors next door were coming. Not having entertained really, I was a bit nervous with the dinner preparations, but all fell into place.

Lord, it is in Your hands. If they ask questions, please guide my answers. My next-door neighbors couldn't come as they were both sick. I was so disappointed but knew the Lord was sovereign. All was well.

The festivities began. The food was good. We even sang a couple of carols at my friend's request. I played some Celtic Christmas fiddle tunes. Then I shared some readings of the Holy Scripture from Abraham's belief in the one, true, living God to the fulfillment of Messiah coming as the lamb in a form of a baby. Then we had Jesus' birthday cake.

Having a birthday cake for Jesus (Yeshua) was a tradition our family had always followed. To my amazement and delight, there was expressed interest in discussing things of God. I knew the Lord had not only answered my heart's cry for "something more" but also had opened the door.

A Faithful God

El Emunah

Know therefore that the LORD your God is God; he is the faithful God, keeping his covenant of love to a thousand generations of those who love him and keep his commandments.

Deuteronomy 7:9

If we are faithless, he will remain faithful, for he cannot disown himself.

2 Timothy 2:13

My birthday was coming up, and I wanted a bicycle. I was going to be six years old. It was time. The day came when my dad said he was going to bring home a bicycle, just for me. I was excited and looking forward to this wonderful gift.

Little did I realize the importance of how getting my first bike would make in my life. In a very clear picturesque way, it set a standard for how I would relate to others as well as my Lord.

I ran from the house, down the steps and on the sidewalk to greet my dad as he got out of the car in front of our house. After greeting me, he pulled the blue bike out of the trunk.

"But, Dad!" I exclaimed! "It's a boy's bike and I'm a girl!" I couldn't understand. Surely, he knew I was a girl and girls had a girl's bike.

He knelt down so he could look me in my eyes and said, "Yes, he knew I was a girl and this was a boy's bike."

Very tenderly, he told me what happened. "Helen, I went to get you a bike at the secondhand store and was happy to see they had two bikes just your size. One was a girl's bike and one was a boy's bike. I was ready to pay for the girl's, when another father came into the store. He too was happy to see a little girl's bike as he was wanting one for his daughter just that size. He said he just had to have the girl's bike as his daughter would be so very upset if she didn't get it."

My loving father said to go ahead and take the girl's bicycle, as he knew I'd be happy with the boy's as well.

I listened to his story and was disappointed, but he was right. I was happy to have a bicycle! They both had two wheels, and that was what I was wanting. I hugged my dad, and he quickly helped me onto the seat and held on as I began to learn to use my bike legs. Oh, what fun! It really didn't matter what gender my bike was for I had my bike.

I'm so very thankful to have learned at such an early age that life was not about me. Perhaps that is why I am not an envious or jealous person. All I know is that was an extremely important lesson for me in learning to put others' needs before my own and in trusting God with how he wants to supply my needs in unexpected but very loving ways.

"Do you have any all-white ones?" I asked.

I was on the phone talking about kittens. I'd seen an ad in the paper for baby Himalayan kittens. I had been introduced to a Himalayan cat many years ago, and I fell in love with it. Blue eyes, long hair, and gentle, yet would follow you around like a dog. It would even retrieve like a dog, and it didn't slobber like a dog, however, *Ha!* Yes, this was the animal for me!

"Yes," she said. "I have three little white ones."

"Oh? How wonderful!" I exclaimed. "How much do you charge for one kitten?"

"Three hundred dollars."

My heart sank. *Three hundred dollars!* Even if I had that much money to spend, I couldn't do it. Wasn't my kind of priority in the whole scheme of things.

"Oh," I said. There is no way I could do that. Then before I knew it, I heard myself asking, "Do you find that sometimes you just can't sell them and give them away?" I was astounded to hear my question.

But she calmly replied. "Well, a couple of times I have had to give them away when I've just too many and can't keep up with all the breeding responsibilities, I've given them to members of my family."

Did I dare ask? Yes, I would.

"If you ever find yourself in that position again, would you think of me?"

"Why, yes, I could do that," she said.

Wow! I gave her my phone number and name and hung up.

It would be a dream come true if that ever happened, I thought. God promises to supply all of our needs. Sometimes He surprises us with giving us our desires, but that was up to Him. I was just thankful God had been so faithful to me in supplying my needs whether a needed job, friend, food, clothing, health, or whatever.

Two to three weeks later, I answered the phone in surprise.

"Why, yes!" I exclaimed. "Two Himalayans would be wonderful. Are they white?"

"No, but they are one-and-a-half years old, and I think one is expecting."

I gasped. I couldn't believe it. *Wow! What fun!* I said to myself.

"When can I get them?" I asked.

"Oh, I'll bring them over in a couple of days."

"Wonderful."

I brought in the chocolate torte Himalayan—what a beauty! The other was the coloring of a Siamese, and she was pregnant. What a sweet cat she was! When she started having contractions a couple of weeks later, she came to tell me! I followed her into my walk-in closet (the only place I hadn't prepared for her to have her kittens) and sat with her as she delivered. How awesome! What a marvel.

She knew just what to do. The first one that was born came out crying. He was so noisy. He was all white and barely as long as my hand stretched out. All seven were born. The closest I ever would come to giving birth. What a miracle! What a delight. I wanted to keep them as long as possible so they would get trained by their mother.

The little white one I named Trouble for he was the instigator of all the kittens' fun. And fun they had! One day while my mother was visiting, she called me to come into the living room to see what was going on. I went in and to my glee saw the mother cat leading all her little kittens up my lambrequin valance and over the window, swinging back and forth as they all went over to the other side and then down the valance.

It was such fun for them and I laughed and laughed! What a gift. What laughter they brought me. What a lovely surprise. God gave me a gift in answering a desire. Oh, how I love Him!

It was sleeting now.

Oh brother, I thought. I'd been driving for four hours in the rain and now it was sleeting. Even though the road was clear-cut, it was new to me, so I was on high alert as it was and now it was sleeting or is it snow. Yikes! First rain, then sleet for about an hour, and now snow! Whew! This was some drive.

I figured it would take me about ten hours to arrive at my destination, and with this weather, I was already tired after five. The snow was starting to pile up. I had to keep going. There was no turn off. Well, this might be a good time to think about what I'd say to the Realtor I was to meet, just to be ready in case everything fell into place.

So I asked myself, what did I want in a house? I laughed as I recalled the verse: "You have not because you ask not." Of course, James says more. "You have not because you have not asked rightly." Surely, if God opened the door for this position, He would want me to have a house that met my needs. So what were my needs?

I thought about the apartments and condos I'd lived in. What were the features I really enjoyed? How many bedrooms? How many bathrooms? As I continued driving in the weather, I found it relaxing to think all this through.

I was single and didn't really have much in the way of furnishings. I was tired of having my car out in the weather, to scrape snow and ice off in the winter. All right, then, I'd like a garage. I'd had two bedrooms before, thinking it would be handy in the event of guests, but guests had come twice in twenty years! I wouldn't need an office, but the option of two bedrooms and two bathrooms seemed best. A screened-in porch would be wonderful. It was something I'd never had, and I knew something I'd really enjoy. Yes, a screened-in porch would be just perfect to enjoy the outdoors and not worry about mosquitoes. A small place always seemed larger with a vaulted ceiling. I sure enjoyed that aspect of my condo. Then there was the fireplace. It was so pleasant to have a crackling fire for a cozy evening. Yes. A fireplace too! Loving flowers the way I do, I added flowerbeds to the list. That would be a wonderful new item for me. Well, now. The list was complete.

It was a good thing, as drivers were being signaled off the road. I pulled over just in front of a four-wheeler. I got out of the car and asked the truck driver to honk when we could get back on the road as I was going to take a nap. I was just about asleep when the honk came.

Well, here we go again. Now the road was a slippery-sliding mess. Cars were all over the place. I asked the Lord for strength and clear thinking and drove on. After ten hours, I was at my destination, exhausted but arriving safely.

The interviewing went on for a couple of days. It was quite an ordeal, quite exhausting. I thought again at how all this came about. I was sure the Lord wanted me to change careers. It had been made so very clear. I remember when a friend at church came up to me and said she wanted to talk with me. We met at her home and she explained the great need for Christian educators. I listened and said that I wasn't looking for a change, as I loved what I was doing as an interior designer. However, if this was of God, I would want to think about it. I went home and that night prayed. I told the Lord that I loved what I was doing, but if He wanted me to become a Christian educator, then I wanted to obey. Only please make it so very clear to me that I couldn't question that it was from Him.

For the past year, I would wake up with a song in my heart. It was a lovely way to wake up. A few days later instead of waking up with a song, I woke up with a small voice saying, "Feed My sheep." Well, I couldn't question that voice. I knew my answer. I now needed to change direction so I could obey my Lord. So here I was with all the interviewing and following the course of events.

I met with the Realtor. I was ready. I mentioned the dollar amount I was able to work with and the features interested in. I walked into "the cottage" and knew that this was it for it had all I had asked God for! The price was right and the features perfect. What a gift from God! "Ask and you shall receive." Well, I had asked and received, so my motive must have been right.

God of My Life

El *Hayyay*

By day the LORD directs his love, at night his song is with me—a prayer to the God of my life.

Psalm 42:8

You killed the author of life, but God raised him from the dead.

Acts 3:15

J ust a few more tugs and that should have it. Yes! The sail was up! I've heard it said that one can do all this by oneself, but I sure don't know how. I could never have put the mast up by myself. It's just too heavy and awkward. But now the sail was up and I was ready to go. Whew! This is no easy feat, pushing this boat into the water. There, one more hard push and I grabbed onto the tarp and jumped on. Quick, get the rudders down into the water. Oh, good, the wind is starting to fill up the sail. I looked back onto the shore and waved to my neighbor. I was off! What a feeling! It was a blue and cloudless sky, sunny and with just enough of a breeze to fill the sail but light enough to give me the illusion I could handle this Hobie Cat. Sigh. What a glorious day!

I was really sailing! I drank in the beauty of the surroundings, the quietness, and the joy that was filling me up. I was overcome with the pleasure of the moment and just had to tell my friend, Jesus, about my feelings. I had learned at a very early age to talk to my friend. Usually it was when I was going through a tough time or was scared or angry about something. This time it was because I was so happy. I've always loved the outdoors and the water. What a special way to enjoy both and have to be quick thinking as well! I really didn't know what I was doing, as I had never sailed a boat before. What a perfect day to start. The wind wasn't all that strong and no one was out on the river. They were all at work. It was my day off, so I could make all kinds of mistakes without pressure! I smiled. It was such a delightful freeing feeling. I sat quietly, drinking in the sunlight.

I was reminded of a boat a long time ago that held some fishermen. In fact, they were friends of my friend Jesus. He was asleep and a storm came up and scared the men. A bit irritated with his sleeping, they woke him up. Taking in the situation, Jesus rebuked the wind, the storm died down, and all was calm again. What a friend! What a lesson!

I could feel the slight wind in the sail as I held onto the line. It was thrilling! It was easy for me to imagine being terrified of a storm out on the water. What a friend I have in Jesus, who cannot only calm a storm out on the water but also calm my troubled heart in the various storms of my own personal life. My weekends were during the week when everybody else was working. It was lonely doing everything alone, but I knew I was never alone because my friend was always with me. He was my joy, my life!

I spread my blanket out on the grass near the few trees and stream of water. I was thankful my friend who'd been here before gave me the good advice to bring a blanket and sweats. It was a lovely fall day, and I was glad to be outside enjoying it.

We were to be back in our "classroom" in the monastery by 5:00 p.m. I didn't have a watch and there were no others close by.

Well, Lord, I don't want to worry about the time, as I really want to take a nap and/or reflect on my life. Will You wake me up if I fall asleep or let me know it's time to go when it is time?

Now time was out of my hands. I could relax and let the Holy Spirit guide me.

I sat down on my blanket and enjoyed looking at the beauty of the colorful leaves. The stream was close by but I didn't hear any movement of the water. Occasionally a bird sang. It was peaceful. It was still. It was quiet. That was why I was here at the quiet, silent monastery. "Be still and know I am God" came to mind.

The Lord had already shown Himself to me in a special way. My cell of a single bed, lamp, nightstand, table, and chair had a clock but the alarm didn't work. I had set the alarm to go off at 3:45 p.m. so I could join the monks at 4:00 a.m. for worship. My alarm didn't go off, and I woke up barely in time for breakfast! The monks were so welcoming in inviting any of us to join in the daily readings at 4:00 a.m., 7:00 a.m., etc., throughout the day and evening readings. I didn't want to miss out. So last night I asked the Holy Spirit to wake me at 3:45 a.m. He did! I jumped out of bed and pulled on my sweats over my pj's to join others in the Cathedral. It was lovely hearing the monks sing the Scripture the way they do. I looked forward to each time of the readings.

My friends at work were quite surprised when I told them I was going to a "silent" monastery. They didn't think I could be quiet. *Ha. Ha.* I told them I was quiet all the time, as I lived alone and hadn't yet begun to talk to myself or answer myself. I was going to the monastery to listen for the voice of God, to learn more about contemplation.

As I lay down on the blanket near the stream and trees, I thought about the beauty of God's creation with the four seasons. There were the buds in the springtime and then the fullness of the plant. Fall brought not only another kind of beauty but also death. As I thought about the cycles of life, I thought about the growth one has spiritually. I thought about the beauty of the changing weather and colors of the leaves. Even the brown ones were pretty. I thought about how in Gods' plan nothing was wasted. He turned what was meant for evil into a blessing when we trusted in Him. Then I fell asleep.

It was barely noticeable at first. Then there it was a bit but such a tiny bit stronger. Then no doubt about it as the gentle breeze brushed my face. Oh, thanks, Holy Spirit. I guess it's time to get up and go to class.

I didn't rush. I felt so refreshed and saw no need to hurry. I silently folded my blanket and leisurely strolled back to our classroom. When I entered the room, I glanced at the clock: 5:00 p.m.

Perfect are the ways of our God, our heavenly and very personal Father.

The LORD Our Peace

Jehovah Shalom

So Gideon built an altar to the LORD there and called it the LORD is Peace.

Judges 6:24

For he himself is our peace, who has made the two one and has destroyed the barrier, the dividing wall of hostility, by abolishing in his flesh the law with its commandments and regulations. His purpose was to create in himself one new man out of the two, thus making peace, and in this one body to reconcile both of them to God through the cross, by which he put to death their hostility. He came and preached peace to you who were far away and peace to those who were near. For through him we both have access to the Father by one Spirit.

Ephesians 2:14-17

I stood by my sliding glass door sipping my tea. I felt so thankful and at peace. Was it just yesterday I'd been offered everything I could ever want on earth?

Just a couple of months ago we'd been introduced by our mutual friend. He wasn't what you'd call handsome, at least I wouldn't say he was, but more like winsome. There was something about him that made you notice him and not his handicap. He asked if I would come to his house, as he'd like to make dinner for me. I agreed so we set a date.

What a beautiful day it was as I drove to his house. His house was in a beautiful setting. Quite a large house with huge old trees scattered throughout a nice green lawn. I could just imagine a time when the women and men would be strolling on the lawn, drinking refreshing lemonade or playing croquet. I sure could see myself playing croquet on that lawn. It was lovely. Close to a Southern plantation from what I remembered from the film *Gone with the Wind*.

I parked my car, opened my door, and walked up to the front door. He greeted me at the door and asked if I'd like a tour of the grounds before we went for a ride on the horses.

"Yes, I would love that."

Off we went. He showed me the guesthouse first, and then we walked over the lovely lawn to his tree house. Unbelievable! It was huge and held a double bed, chair, and television. *Is he a romantic?* I wondered. It sure touched my romantic heart. What a fun place it would be to sleep in the summer nights. What a huge treehouse! What a large tree! We climbed down the ladder of the tree house and walked over to the water where his sailboat sat tied to a pier. No small boat like mine but a nice sloop. She had beautiful lines. I didn't say much but let him give me the tour and took it all in. Then he showed me the tennis court and then the lap pool. Wow! What next?

As if in answer to my question, he led me to his barn, and we saddled up the horses. It was a nice easy ride. I was beyond curious, so I asked him.

"What happened to your arm?" The answer sent chills up my back as I could identify with his story only too well.

"I ran in front of a school bus when I was in kindergarten."

I could barely breathe when I took in the story, for I had been a kindergarten teacher and was always nervous when the children were getting on the buses after school let out.

"It certainly didn't keep you from living a normal life," I said.

He went on to explain that after that accident he was sent away to learn how to live with one arm.

He had learned well, I thought.

After our ride, he fixed a nice meal. He could do everything! I didn't even notice his handicap. Then the time came for the tour of his mansion, as it was no small house. He had a theater room and a bowling room besides a library. Then he said he'd like to take me flying in his airplane. We set a date. While walking me to my car, we saw some of his goats. It was the first time I'd been up close to a goat and was intrigued by the eyes. I've loved them ever since.

A few weeks later, he flew over to the little airport near my condo to take me flying. We were to fly to a historic little island and have lunch. He must be a romantic! What a delightful idea for a date! I hadn't had much breakfast and was that a mistake. It was a turbulent ride.

We landed and enjoyed walking into the little town for lunch. Soon we were flying again. The ride was worse going back, and my unsettled stomach reacted just as we were starting to land. He noticed my discomfort and quickly handed me a pail as he smoothly landed the plane. I was touched with his concern and care. I had never reacted to flying before. I loved to fly, and I remember the very first time I flew I was disappointed not to use the bag that was supplied for just a reason. Why now? I was embarrassed, but he was so sweet about it all.

He said it was my turn to choose what to do. So as we said good-bye I mentioned going to the zoo.

It turned out to be another clear, beautiful day. He was so easy to be with. So intelligent and well read.

I could really fall for this man, I thought as we strolled along enjoying the animals.

Then he asked me. He wanted someone to fly and travel with him. How I'd love that! As we talked, I realized there was more that he expected. I mentioned being just friends. He said he had enough friends. I was saddened, for there was no spiritual understanding. He had everything I could possibly want on this earth. We said good-bye, and I knew I'd never see him again.

I walked back to my kitchen and put my teacup down. He may have offered me the "world" as I enjoyed absolutely everything he had, but he was lacking one thing. He lacked the peace that I have—peace that passes all understanding and gives joy, not just a fleeting happiness. I felt so rich, content, and at peace.

Smiling, I washed and dried my teacup, for I knew the Prince of Peace.

God My Exceeding Joy

El Simchath Gili

Yet I will rejoice in the LORD, I will be joyful in God my Savior.

Habakkuk 3:18

Jesus said, "As the Father has loved me, so have I loved you. I have told you this so that my joy may be in you and that your joy may be complete."

John 15:9, 11

"Oh, come on! Let's play it seven times instead of the regular three as tradition did," I said, laughingly.

It was my turn to choose the tune, and as usual, I chose my favorite Irish tune. I was the only female in our Scottish fiddle group, and the other five members kindly humored me in agreeing to play the tune more than the normal three times. My fingers flew into place on the strings. It was a fun tune.

Sometimes our guitarist would speed up the rhythm, and I would find myself grinning as we all tried to keep up. What fun we had getting together once a month, trying our best to sound as wonderful as the Celtic tunes did on the CDs we would listen to. This was something I looked forward to every month. I was so thankful that my dream of being in a fiddle group was now a reality.

My thoughts went back to when I'd first gotten my violin. I was five years old and had been asking for a violin for three years. My interest had started when my mother played a record that was more of a teaching platform on various instruments. Mother majored in music in college, so she wanted her children to also share her interest in music. We all did. I chose the violin, but it took three years to persuade my parents I was serious.

My first teacher was wonderful. He was such a kind, gentle man that got me off to an excellent start. I loved practicing and went through my lesson material quickly. He said I had a good ear. I was a very fast learner. But one day when I arrived for my weekly lesson, he wasn't there. We found out he had died suddenly, perhaps a heart attack. Oh, how I missed him. Then the hunt began for a new teacher. She was a lovely lady, and I began lessons with her when around seven years old after about one and a half years with my first teacher.

Our family moved a couple of times during my youth, and this affected me in my playing the violin. Bad habits were acquired and, yes, even some bad attitude. I remember once being so angry with my last violin teacher in high school that I paid him in loose pennies! I'd had it. However, I once got to go to a violin camp and had a wonderful time playing with others. This was a new experience that made all the constant practice enjoyable. There was no high school or college orchestra to enjoy. My violin collected dust during college days and much was forgotten after so much hard work.

However, my love for the violin did not diminish. I found myself picking it up and playing once again but only for pleasure. Eventually, I began to forget the finger positions of all seven positions, so I would play hymns as worship just between me and my God. It was special.

Then one day, unexpectedly, I went to a new church where they had an orchestra. It was a very large congregation of about five thousand at that time. I decided to see if I would be welcomed in the orchestra having lost so much of what I'd learned. Was God's spirit of love evident or was performance more important? I wondered. I went one night to a practice and was kindly welcomed. So few were there, and I couldn't hide my playing among the players. The acting conductor, a professional clarinet player, asked me how long I'd been playing. Not knowing he was a professional but fully aware of my terrible playing (or was it screeching), I said I started when I was five. I loved him instantly when he didn't miss a beat and invited me to come back. Probably to his great surprise, I did and happily I began remembering and playing much better. What a joy it was to be part of an orchestra!

I moved again. It was in an area of mountain music. One day, I heard of a weeklong camp for fiddlers.

That's what I want, I thought. *I've lost too much of my classical training, and anyway I'm a proud Scot, so that's what I'll do.*

"How about 'Margaret's Waltz,'" I said. It was time to end our session, and traditionally 'Margaret's Waltz' was played, so we played it that night.

Life can be so full of twists and turns. I was so thankful God had guided me as I sought to fulfill my dream of playing the violin. Or was it the fiddle I wanted all along!

She called saying how cold it was, walking to work this winter. I knew immediately what I needed to do. I should have done it this summer when the thought crossed my mind. I certainly wasn't using it. I'd been wearing the coat maybe once a year and that was a real maybe. I'd probably used it five times since buying it. I found a box after repairing a tear, folded it up, and mailed it the next day. A huge smile filled my face. What a wonderful surprise it will be. It was already a terribly cold winter. Not just a bitter cold but also a real polar cold with lots of snow. My coat would be perfect for her.

I remember when I saw the black, long, bunny-fur coat in a consignment store I occasionally visited. I don't like coats. I once had a raincoat that was blue and had some pleats in the back. It was a one-of-a-kind and so very stylish. I enjoyed every minute wearing it. I had hoped to enjoy it the rest of my life, but someone liked it too and took it. This black bunny was such a classic cut and was so soft. *No*, I thought. *I don't really look good in black.* So I walked away.

Over the year I would drop in the store to see if there might be a good bargain and glance at the coat from afar. Then one day while shopping I decided to see if it would fit. Why not? Just for fun. I put it on and, lo and behold, it fit as if it was made for me.

It so rarely gets cold enough here for a fur coat, I thought. But the price was more than a bargain! Why not! I could always wear it downtown when we celebrate the opening of Christmas shopping the first weekend in December. It might be cool enough then if I wear light clothing. So I bought it and smiled all the way home.

I enjoyed wearing the black bunny. I felt elegant and playful at the same time! Someone thought it a mink! Yes, I had enjoyed it, but it was truly needed and would look absolutely delightful on her with her black hair, height, and trim figure! Thanks, Lord, for giving me the opportunity to hold on loosely to something so beautiful, warm, and needed.

There, I did it! I felt lighter, freer. I smiled to myself. So that's what the Lord was preparing me to do, I thought. How wonderful! I'd just given away my 35-mm camera with its additional telephoto lens, wide-angle lens, filters, and carrying case. It had been an unexpected gift from my dad. He knew the joy of taking pictures and really had an artistic eye for it. Wanting his children to have such a pleasure, he gave us cameras. I guess it was my turn. I really hadn't thought about it, although I had mentioned getting a simple little camera as I was going on a college study trip for a month to Paris, Rome, Geneva, and Florence to study fine art. As if that wasn't enough, Dad gave me twenty-four rolls of 35-mm film to use on my trip! Dad said to me as I packed that I couldn't come back till I had used up all the film. Wow! How freeing is that! What a gift of love to me for I knew he would have liked to have such a gift for himself. So off I went clicking away on my delightful trip!

For some reason, the one picture I had in mind that I really had to take was French bread being carried home by some Frenchman. We arrived in Paris first and were there for five days at least. However, I never saw anyone carrying French bread! But not to be discouraged, I thought there still would be a possibility, as we would return a few days before going back to the United States. Sure enough on the last day of the trip, I spotted someone caring three loaves of French bread! I used some French to get the young boy's attention.

It was a rainy day. *No wonder they make the crust so hard*, I thought. Perhaps it will still have some semblance of crust when he gets home. I took my picture, thanked him, and went to my hotel to get my suitcase and leave. *Sure hope it turns out*, I mused.

To my delight, it did and Dad presented me with a blown-up picture of my "blue boy," as I called it as he was dressed all in blue. Dad also presented me with another blown-up and framed picture of Moses I had taken in the Westminster Cathedral. I wasn't sure I'd get it, as it was so dark and needed a flash, as I didn't have one.

But to my amazement, it did and I have to credit that to others that took flash pictures just as I clicked my camera. I think Dad was especially proud of that picture of Moses, for he and Mom had been there, but his picture of Moses didn't turn out. What a most wonderful gift that camera was.

It is so interesting how giving my camera away had come about. I had been thinking about how we need to hold onto a thing loosely, for that is how God can use us to bless others. As I lay in bed, quiet and still, I often find I hear God leading me in my thoughts. One night I found myself thinking about my camera. I'd recently met someone who was artistic and was wondering if there was something

I could do to encourage her. Was giving my camera the answer? Then the answer came in a most unexpected and delightful way.

My neighbor had died, and I was invited to come for a buffet dinner after the memorial service with other neighbors who were friends. I had been a partial caregiver to him in that I'd transport him each day to see his wife in an assisted-living place and do a couple of other errands for him from time to time. I called Mothers' caregiver that came on Wednesday nights to join me, as she'd helped out with him on my behalf a few times. She was thrilled to join me that evening as she'd enjoyed him as well. He just missed his one-hundredth-birthday celebration by two months. As we sat eating and visiting, I suddenly felt compelled to ask if her son had a camera.

"No, not really," she said. He'd had a class in college in which he was able to use the colleges' cameras. Her son was very artistic and majoring in art. Here was my answer!

"Please don't tell him who it came from—if anything, tell him it came from the Lord." I said.

How true that was, I thought, for the Lord prompted me to give my camera away. We are to hold onto things loosely. Yes, I felt lighter, freer, and more able to focus on my Lord God. A little of what it is to die to oneself.

I remembered a story I'd told my nieces and nephew when their dad, my brother, died, how one day this young man was walking along a path and came upon a man carrying a load on his back. This wise man asked the young man if he wanted to come with him as he was going to see the king.

Why yes, said the young man so they went along together for a while. Then the young man saw a place he liked and decided to settle for a little time. The wise man said good-bye and continued on his journey to the king.

The young man built a house and lived there for some time. Then he remembered he could go see the king, for the king was having a celebration. So he sold his house and started on his way to the king. Sometimes he would pick up things on his way, but the load on his back would get heavy and slow him down, so he'd give those things away, and his steps became lighter, and he felt less burdened.

Joy began to fill him more and more as he journeyed toward the castle. As he saw the king's castle from a distance, he put down anything he was carrying so he could run to the king and join in on the celebration.

Yes, there is a time for everything, and now was the time to hold loosely my things I had so enjoyed and let them go as the Holy Spirit led me.

God Our Hope

O Israel, put your hope in the LORD, for with the LORD is unfailing love and with him is full redemption.

Psalm 130: 7

Command those who are rich in this present world not to be arrogant nor to put their hope in wealth, which is so uncertain, but to put their hope in God, who provides us with everything for our enjoyment.

1 Timothy 6:17

Saying good-bye is never easy. Growing up as I did, I had learned to say good-bye at an early age. It wasn't easy then, and it isn't easy now. Moving every few years taught me how to make friends quickly, and then there was the inevitable good-bye. With some of those friends, I've managed to stay in contact. After losing contact with a couple of my closest friends for twenty years, somehow we made contact again and what a wonderful blessing it has been to me!

But this time it was different. My head was muddled with so many thoughts. My heart was full of so many feelings. It was awful. I didn't want to talk about it, and I did want to talk about it. Others didn't know how to talk about it with me. I needed to feel the sadness and pain of saying good-bye for the last time. She and I hadn't always gotten along. She was my sister. She was the oldest one in the family. She was the one who by placement of birth had more responsibility put upon her. She didn't always want me around. I looked up to her. Not only was she full of life and fun, always coming up with a great idea for something to do, but also she was beautiful and extremely talented. She'd had it tougher socially than I had had. I don't know why; life just isn't fair.

In the last couple of years, I had so enjoyed our times together. Instead of quietly competing with one another, we at last were enjoying the uniqueness of the other's personality and abilities. It was fun being her sister. I remember the excitement of her wedding. It was like a fairytale story in how they met. I couldn't help but be happy for her. She had waited such a long time to marry. It wasn't easy having her marry and then get whisked off to another country to live. Not only did she have a new husband to adjust to but also a new country and whole new way of life.

Then the news came. It was Hodgkin's disease.

"Oh no, Lord, why her? She just got married! I'm still single—why not me?" My heart was so heavy. I wrote her every week. One night I woke up. I was sure she had been calling my name.

"Oh, Lord," I cried. What is it? What is it you want me to pray for her? You can do anything. I pray you heal her."

Then I went to see her. She wanted to talk about dying. I just couldn't. I let her down when she needed me most. It's never easy saying good-bye, not when you love someone.

Then I smiled. I can say good-bye for now, what blessed relief to know I will someday see you again. You are with the Lord. Where there is no pain, or sadness, or sorrow, or sickness, or loneliness. You are where there is only *joy*. You are with the Lord, and someday I will see you again.

How utterly desolate it must be to say good-bye to someone you love when you have no assurance of the hope set before you in the life and death and resurrection of Jesus the Messiah.

A Teacher Come from God

Now there was a man of the Pharisees named Nicodemus, a member of the Jewish ruling council. He came to Jesus at night and said, "Rabbi, we know you are a teacher who has come from God. For no one could perform the miraculous signs you are doing if God were not with him.

John 3:1, 2

Jesus replied, "If anyone loves me, he will obey my teaching"

John 14:23

I called the local newspaper to see if they would be interested in our story.

"Wonderful! I'll make sure the team is here so you can take our picture. Would it be possible to have two pictures? I think you will understand why when you get here. See you then," I said.

What a joyful experience it had been. How delightful and useful, it had turned out. The room was finished. Instead of a drab, lifeless gray, it now was transformed into a place the children would be happy to call their own—a place they could worship and learn about God the Father, God the Son, and God the Holy Spirit. I certainly had enjoyed the process.

Wanting to do something other than the normal trend of the time, I asked the Lord to guide me in my thoughts. Did I want a Noah's ark painted on the wall like so many churches? No, because I'd already painted one on my huge wall to add some color and interest as well as distinction of my office being the Christian education office. What was the purpose I was trying to accomplish? Would it be useful for educating? Would it be a delight to the eyes? Would the children feel ownership? How could we keep the interest going? Certainly, we wouldn't want the children to walk into the room without expectation of something new as time went by. How could we accomplish that?

I had asked the Lord to bring artists into my life that would be willing to take the project on. Then, having discovered another woman and two men, we made up our team. Praying my way through as I tried to stir up their creative juices and lead them to the result I envisioned, we began.

It was a ten-month project to create our temple. It was so enjoyable working together, shopping together, and gathering ideas of how best to create the space. One day, we took a day trip to visit some frescoes in the area. One of the men was a very fine, notable painter. We couldn't have accomplished our vision without him. One man was the nuts-and-bolts guy. He made sure our ideas would work. The other woman was our Biblical research person. She checked out Scripture to make sure we chose colors accordingly.

The children were excited. They got involved and made handprints to help in the understanding of the outer court. Fabric was hung to divide the outer and inner courts. What beautiful fabric it was! Props were purchased to aid in telling and acting out Bible stories. Pictures of Old and New Testament stories were painted and hung in place. They would be removed and changed for new ones to keep the children interested and observant. The Ark of the Covenant was made to be put behind our Holy of Holies place with a torn curtain in front and a picture of a lit up cross behind. Cushions were sewn for the children to sit on during teaching-storytelling time. We even had a little podium made so the children that could read could take turns standing behind it and read our Bible Scripture for our lesson. We laughed together as were worked hard to accomplish our purpose. It was a most enjoyable experience for all involved. It was the most enjoyable and satisfying experience of my life.

Our pictures were taken. Two pictures were put into the paper with a noteworthy article. I was so pleased. We dedicated our temple to God. The children were all eyes and ears. They were so eager to worship in their own temple. We took off our shoes as it was holy ground. Spiritual growth was being nurtured. We had just begun. What a great beginning.

I will praise the LORD no matter what happens. I will constantly speak of his glories and grace. I will boast of all his kindness to me. Let all who are discouraged take heart. Let us praise the LORD together, and exalt his name.

Psalm 34: 1-4

To obey is better than sacrifice.

1 Samuel 15:22

A favorite song of mine, and one that my dad would sing to me as a child when we went driving somewhere together, is "Trust and Obey." This hymn was inspired when a young man was heard saying, "I am not quite sure, but I am going to trust, and I am going to obey." The young man had just heard Dwight L. Moody preach about living a Christian life. Daniel B. Towner sent the quote to John H. Sammis, a minister, who wrote the refrain and stanzas. Daniel B. Towner set the words to music in 1887.

TRUST AND OBEY

When we walk with the Lord
In the light of His Word,
What a glory He sheds on our way!
While we do His good will,
He abides with us still,
And with all who will trust and obey.
REFRAIN
Trust and obey, for there's no other way
To be happy in Jesus, but to trust and obey.

Not a shadow can rise,
Not a cloud in the skies,
But His smile quickly drives it away;
Not a doubt or a fear, not a sigh or a tear,
Can remain when we trust and obey.
REFRAIN
Not a burden we bear,
Not a sorrow we share,
But our toil He doth richly repay;
Not a grief or a loss,
Not a frown or a cross,
But is blest if we trust and obey.
REFRAIN
Then in fellowship sweet,
We will sit at His feet.
Or we'll walk by His side in the way;
What He says we will do,
Where He sends we will go,
Never fear, only trust and obey.
REFRAIN
Trust and obey, for there's no other way,
To be happy in Jesus, but to trust and obey.

This is a song deep within my heart and one I have found so true. I think the words say just what it means when one truly does trust and obey the Lord. Yes, yes, and yes again, Jehovah God is TRUSTworthy!

Printed in the United States
By Bookmasters